A GIFT FOR:

_____

FROM:

_____

Published by Hallmark Gift Books,
a division of Hallmark Cards, Inc.,
Kansas City, MO 64141
Visit us on the Web at Hallmark.com.

Editorial Director: Delia Berrigan
Editor: Theresa Trinder
Art Director: Chris Opheim
Designer: Brian Pilachowski
Production Designer: Dan Horton

ISBN: 978-1-63059-831-0
BOK1063
Made in China
0518

Ready to Give No Damns

Loving, Living, and Laughing Like You Mean It

BY Melvina Young

Hallmark

Show Yourself Some Love

There are so many things out there waiting to kick our asses as women. You know what I mean—job demands, family needs, friendship commitments, and those things we feel obligated to do from pure love. (Not complaining. Just explaining.)

If you include community, school, and church responsibilities or sneak in our personal improvement, health, and fitness goals, and then add on the pressure from millions and millions of mouths in media and social media explaining to us how we're doing it all wrong . . . some self-love starts to sound pretty good, doesn't it?

From time to time I like to give myself a little quiz:

Question 1: Why should I help the universe kick my own ass?

Question 2: Shouldn't I be on my own side?

(Answers: "I shouldn't!" and "Hell yes!")

That's why I consider myself a whole-souled woman. Because a whole-souled woman is a woman who performs—if not perfects—the art of self-love. A whole-souled woman accepts herself even as she works to be better. A whole-souled woman knows to throw up the deuces at all the pressures and the mess and find peace with herself. She figures out what she needs. And then she sets about building herself the way she wants.

For me, that's meant making my mistakes, having my sorrows, sometimes second-guessing myself, but always trying to treat myself like my own best friend. I can honor the wise part of me that knows a woman's worth is the most valuable thing she can take ownership of. And I can own the dumbass part of me that steps on the scale three to five times to try to trick physics into showing me a slightly lower number.

I am a big defender and protector of me, just as I am with everyone I love and care for. And that's what it's all about: loving yourself, your whole self, no matter what. It's about having your own back and being in your own corner.

I live by several mantras—those little things you say to yourself that act like guideposts, those sayings you hold deep in your belief system that keep you anchored:

Mess up. Own it. Move on. Grow.

This woman is guilt-free.

Love is my super power.

*It's called "practicing kindness"
because we're meant to get better at it.*

*A woman only "lets herself go"
because she's holding everyone else together.*

These are my mission statements in life. Taken together, they could be my autobiography.

And I'm sharing my mantras (and my mission) with you because I want you to love you, too. I want us, as women, to feel like we're enough. I want us to reject words like "flaws" or ideas like "being a bad friend" or a "bad mom" or a "bad" anything. I want us to find more things to like and admire about ourselves. I want us to love us for our excellence and for our imperfections, too. I want to encourage us to look at ourselves and love who we see.

I want to convince us that it's OK. It's all perfectly OK to be less than 100% perfect and 100% everything to everybody. It's OK.

This book is for when you need inspiration, encouragement, a laugh, or just a reminder that you're good, just like you are.

YOU DOWN?

Let's do this.

I AM

a whole-
souled
woman.

BRAVE:

When everybody takes a seat but you're still standing.

LOVE
like you mean it.

EVERY WOMAN
WHO EVER FLEW
STARTED WITH
a leap of faith.

WHEN A

grown Woman

SPEAKS—

TAKE YOUR SEAT.

Obey Mama...

AND EVERYBODY
GETS OUT
OF THIS ALIVE.

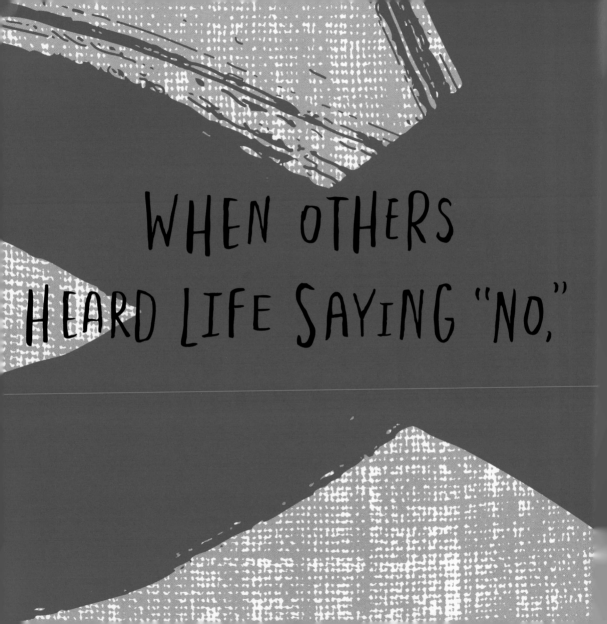

WHEN OTHERS
HEARD LIFE SAYING "NO,"

SHE HEARD
"JUST NOT RIGHT NOW."

I believe the word you're looking for is

"BOLD."

JUDGES

ARE FOR COURTROOMS.

LEAN ON THE PEOPLE WHO **LOVE you** UNCONDITIONALLY.

STRENGTH
IS KNOWING THAT

It's OK TO BE

FRAGILE

SOMETIMES.

Sometimes I feel like asking the universe,

"Will this be on the exam?"

UP TO ANYONE ELSE,
I had to
stand up to
MYSELF.

I know myself by heart.

Will Work for Joy

I live for laughter. I work hard for joy. I love love, both giving and receiving it. And I try to feed every part of my soul with these things because they are the essence of life.

So maybe that makes me sound like I've had the kind of life where hard things don't happen. But nothing could be further from the truth.

I live for laughter, work hard for joy, and love love because hard things have happened. I am a clinical depression survivor. I've lost people who anchored me to this earth. And I have a daughter, my only child, the center of my universe, who suffers with a debilitating illness she will have all of her life.

I have lived in anger, and I have resided in grief. But here is what I've found: when life hands me a cupped palm full of grief, I can, in time, force its fingers open to look for understanding, wisdom, hope, and yes—even joy.

See, when I was lost in the solid darkness of depression, the misfiring chemistry of my brain and the trials of life colluded to make sure that I could only achieve two emotions: profound sadness and deep nothingness.

I had to develop a practice of thorough self-care and intense self-protection just to keep going—to get up every day, to keep moving, to keep living. And I promised myself that if I were ever allowed to feel joy again, I was going to grab it and hang on to it like a life raft on the high rolling seas.

And, luckily for me, after five seemingly infinite years, the dark night of depression slowly dissolved and the light came back. The first thing I did when I took note of the dawn was to go searching for joy. And I began to find it. And it saved me. That's why I'm serious—even militant—about joy.

For me, joy can be found in the smallest of things: my daughter's sunlit laughter, my spouse's handsome smile, a "good news" story where a random person does a random good just to make the world feel better, an uninterrupted ten minutes to and for myself, a kitten video.

Oh, and a Christmas tree in every room of my little house at Christmastime. Or a Christmas tree in my living room in May. Or July. My house. My tree. My choice. My joy.

Now. I'm not promising you that pursuing joy will mean that you'll be happy all the time. That's not real life. Purposefully pursuing joy means that the possibility to feel happiness exists because you make room for it.

That's my commitment to finding and honoring joy. And it's made my soul more whole each day. I wish that for you, too.

EVERYTHING I NEED IS RIGHT HERE.

No Matter How Many Times I Think I've

LOST MY WAY,
THIS IS WHERE I'M
SUPPOSED TO BE.

LOVE
IS MY
SUPER
POWER.

I WILL KEEP
doing me.

No Permission Slip Necessary.

IT'S CALLED
"practicing kindness"
BECAUSE WE'RE MEANT TO GET BETTER AT IT.

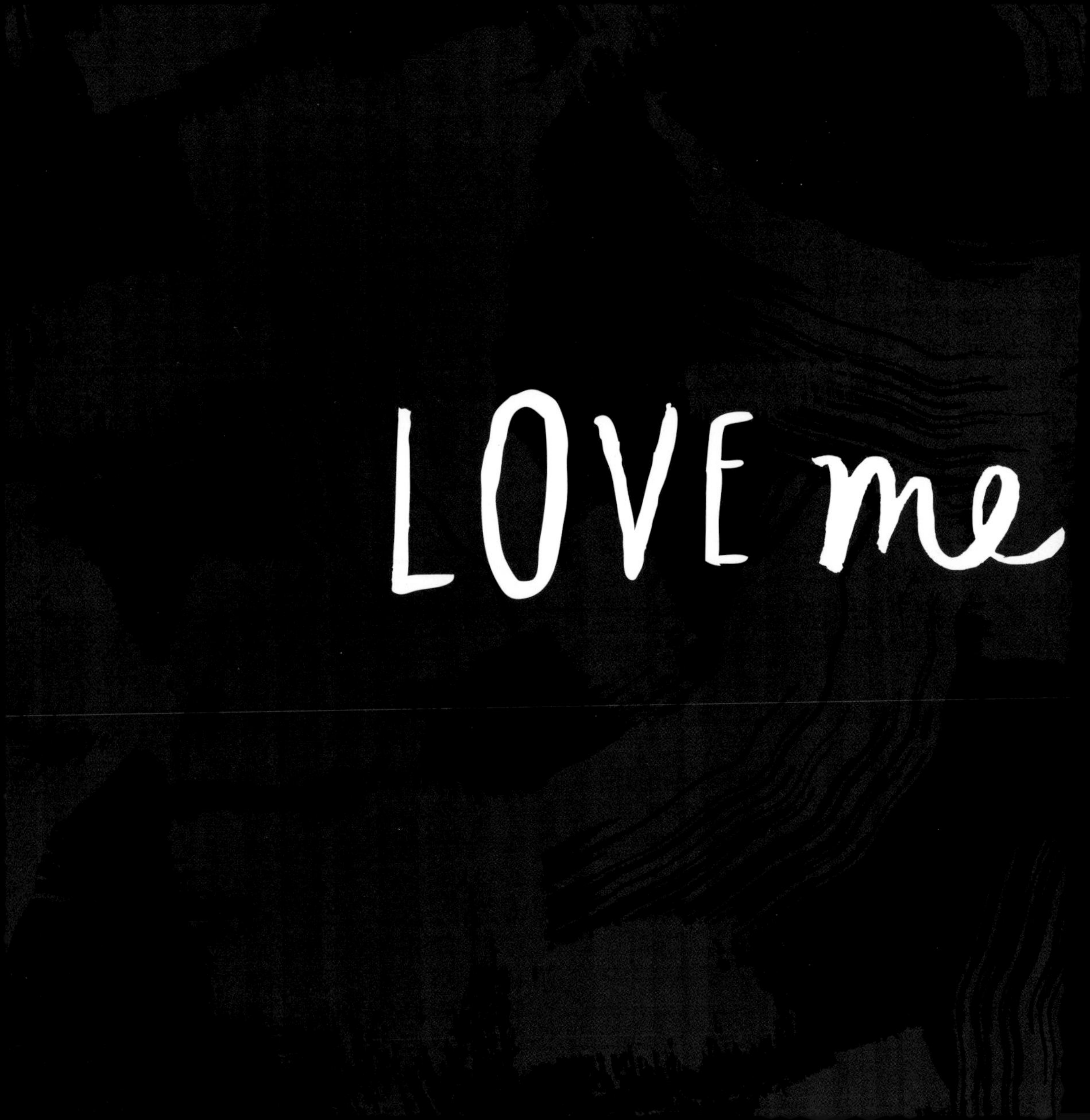
LOVE me

SOME ME.

♥

SELF-*love*

IS not
SELF-*ish*.

IF I COULD GO BACK IN TIME, I WOULD TELL MYSELF,

"YOU GOT THIS."

If you don't have anything **NICE** to say to yourself,

Don't Say ANYTHING at All.

I TEACH
PEOPLE HOW TO
LOVE ME

by how I
love me.

♥

THE UNIVERSE IS wide.

YOU WILL FIND YOUR PLACE IN IT.

I can.
I will.
I did.

ONCE I KICKED

my inner

BULLY'S BUTT,

I RAN AROUND
LIFE'S
playground
WITH JOY.

Never Let Yourself Go

Don't you just hate when women let themselves go? Wait! Where are you going?

Trust me. I understand the urge to run away screaming and pulling out your weave when you hear that. Because we get it all the time, don't we? And not just from the guys—from ourselves, too.

Whether we're running our 15,013th errand of the day, frantically trying to do something for somebody who needs it now, or trying to get in the day's workout before the night's dinner, there are SO MANY things to worry about! Should how we look really be the most important one of them? Here's a hint: Nope.

So, I promise—this is not another judgy thing about how if you gain ten pounds you've utterly betrayed your partner, set a bad example for your children, and caused the downfall of western civilization. Or how if you dare experience the passage of time and start to look a day older, you're insulting everybody with 20/20 vision.

I understand. I swear sometimes as I'm rushing out the door with one shoe in my hand, my bag slung over my shoulder, and my outfit barely "slung" together, it feels like RuPaul is standing behind me yelling, "You better work!" And all I can think is "Shut up! I'm working as hard as I can!"

Don't get me wrong. A whole-souled woman like myself has got the vanity! She takes pride in looking fly and in completing all the rituals that make her feel that way. But she knows that her beauty is about a lot more than how she looks. It's about what she does, what she knows, how she acts, and who she is to herself and other people.

Beauty is not a mask to wear for other people's approval. Beauty is not "working" what you're wearing. Beauty is working who you really are, loving it, and then being bold enough to expect other people to love it, too.

So when I say "Don't let yourself go, girl!" I mean don't lose the "you" in who you are. Don't let go of the woman—the self—you've worked so hard to be.

I know. That's a challenge in the real world when everything in our lives demands that we put ourselves dead last on our own to-do lists. With only twenty-four hours in the day, by the time we get everything done for everybody else, there might be three minutes and thirty-seven seconds (total) left for ourselves.

This is what being a modern woman means. We love our families, all the people we care for and do for. We do. And we're committed to our jobs inside and outside the house. But, even when we're intentionally working on ourselves, it's still too easy to let ourselves go.

So, here's my short list for how to put yourself higher on your own to-do list:

Don't let yourself go last.

Don't let yourself go crazy with stress.

Don't let yourself go bananas with guilt.

Don't let yourself go over the edge with commitments.

Don't let yourself go without the self-love you need and the self-care you deserve.

Hold you. Love you. Be gentle with you. Use tender words with you. Schedule some time for you—even if it's just a few minutes a day. Grab that time. Hoard that time. Protect that time.

And when the people who depend on you come knocking, calling, or crying, be ready to say, "I'm busy not letting myself go so that I can keep you all together!"

NOW FEATURING "ME"

AT THE TOP OF MY TO-DO LIST.

EACH TIME
SHE STOOD UP
FOR HERSELF,

HER LEGS
grew stronger.

Know your mind.

SPEAK IT.

DO
WHAT YOU CAN
AND FAKE THE REST.

Sometimes a "NO" to someone else is a "YES" to me.

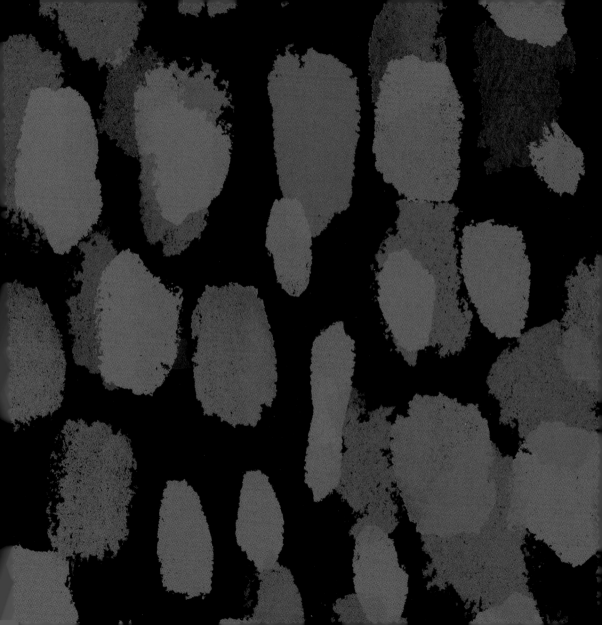

You may Ignore The Queen.

But, she's still
The Queen.

THIS Woman IS GUILT-FREE.

GRACE IS OUR REMINDER THAT OUR HEARTS

YOU ONLY
"let yourself go"

WHEN YOU'RE HOLDING EVERYONE ELSE TOGETHER.

THE PATH TO HAPPINESS IS PAVED WITH A LOT OF

"I don't give a damns."

DEAR UNIVERSE,
If you have
a drama-free
moment
planned for me,

I'd like to redeem it NOW.

RISE.
Kick ass.

Rest.
Repeat.

Imperfection Rules!

I am an imperfect woman. I'm good with that because I've figured out something important: I am enough. And so are you. You're good, just like you are.

You don't need to lose another five pounds to be perfect. You don't need to focus on your "problem areas" to be happier. Maybe you had a baby and the little angel put a little leftover "pot" on your belly. But why is that a problem? (You know guys get bellies from beer, right? You incubated a whole human!)

You don't need to spend your last dime exfoliating "old" skin to look "new." Because guess what? Time is real and unstoppable, and next week it'll just be "old" again.

So how about we give ourselves something I like to call a freakin' break. It's time to stop killing ourselves over "perfect." (Remember that thing about not helping the universe put its boot in our butts?)

OK, so maybe you'll never get your house "simplified" or organized to Martha Stewart's expectations. Maybe your thighs have a couple of dimples you think would look cuter on your face. Maybe you let your kid eat a Twinkie and now you're worrying that this one single thing is going to knock him down from Harvard to Hank's Clown College and Car Wash.

But guess what? Martha Stewart ain't your mama! She's not coming by to check under your couch for handcrafted dust bunnies. Dimples are nature's smile wherever they are. And your kid will be fine. Twinkies are full of preservatives. Preservatives preserve things. Boom! You just increased your kid's longevity. Good job.

Look, I'm not saying to lie down on the couch and let nature reclaim your house and your body. I'm saying that maybe it's time to admit that all the things the world asks of us aren't things we have to give. Maybe it's time to relax, take a deep breath, and embrace our status as whole-souled women.

Because a whole-souled woman loves and accepts herself, just like she is. She's imperfect (also known as real) and she's satisfied with that. Does she work on improving herself? Hells yeah! If she's good, then she can only get better. But "perfect" is dead to her. Dead.

Yes. A whole-souled woman's got her "stuff" just like anybody. But she's become her own best defender instead of her own worst critic. She'll take off her earrings and put on her boxing gloves in defense of who she is and who she is becoming.

She's come to own the power of self-love and understands the freedom that comes with learning to laugh at herself and shake off what every. single. body. else thinks of her.

So if this is you, or you want it to be you, guess what? You're a whole-souled woman. Recognize it. Own it. Work it. Unleash it on the world.

Ready
to give
No
DAMNS.

Consider the sexy brought.

I OWN MY
Sh*t.

I PAID ENOUGH FOR IT.

I kick ass.

I COME BACK
FOR NAMES
LATER.

Do Not
MAKE MY
"CUSSER"
COME ON.

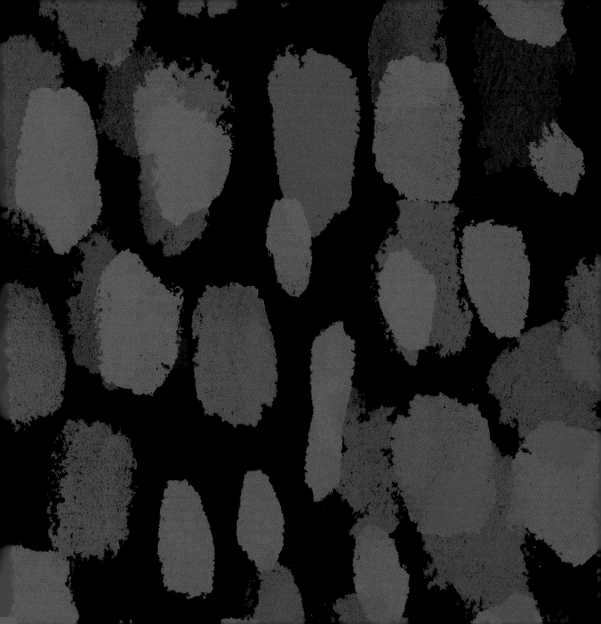

IS IT HOT IN HERE OR IS IT JUST ME?

Damn right it's ME.

A whole-souled woman

LOOKS BETTER
ACCIDENTALLY
THAN MOST
PEOPLE DO
ON PURPOSE.

I'm the Funniest thing

I'VE LAUGHED AT ALL DAY.

I SLAY DRAGONS DAILY.
AND MY SWEATPANTS
ARE NEVER SINGED.

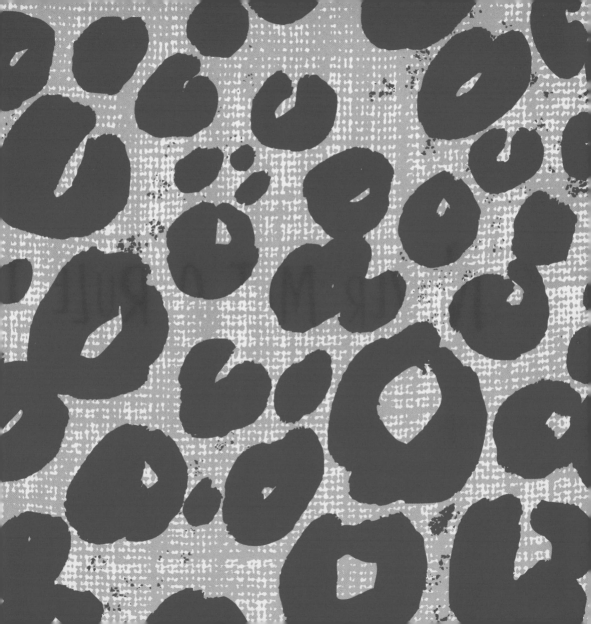

NEVER MET A RULE I

COULDN'T SET ON FIRE.

I DON'T WORRY ABOUT WHAT MY *ass* LOOKS LIKE.

It's always behind ME.

MESS UP.

Own it.

MOVE ON.

grow.

I AM SENDING ME AN UNCONDITIONAL LOVE LETTER:

"Dear Self,
thanks for
becoming
YOU."

About the Author

Melvina Young grew up in "The Woods" in Lepanto, Arkansas, surrounded by a loving family with a gift for singing, storytelling, and laughing—even through hard times. She fell in love with words and writing from the moment her mother helped her trace the alphabet and whispered "Imagine" in her ear.

Now a writer for Hallmark, Melvina gets to share her passion for spreading empathy, compassion, and love every day. When Melvina is not writing words of hope and optimism for Hallmark, she's figuring out ways to help people connect more deeply and get along better. When she's not working on world peace, a lecture, or a blog post, she's enjoying German wine, Dutch cheese, Belgian chocolate, or hip-hop dance class.

Acknowledgments

Special thanks to and for my partner in life, Greg Streich, and our daughter, Sage, the real reason I do anything. More special thanks to my mother, Sadie Young, who reacts to each word I write like she did with the first one I ever wrote all by myself. Big thanks to the Hallmark team who believed in this project and worked so hard to help it live, especially Mary Gentry, Will Brown, Brian Pilachowski, and most especially my homegirl, Lauren Miller, who kept seeing bigger and better things for my writing. And, last but never least, a big special thanks to Theresa Trinder, my clear-eyed editor and truth-telling friend.